MW01173781

Dear Atlas
It's Me, Your Dad

Letters from an Expecting Dad

By Aaron Plaat

Contents

Introduction

When I was younger, I often skipped reading book introductions in an effort to get to the "good stuff" right away. With age comes wisdom, and I eventually realized the introduction provides important context for every book, no matter how small.

I now see the introduction as a way to understand the author before reading their book. Who are they? What helped contribute to their message? Most of this can be found in the book introduction.

Who am I? Nobody special. I was born into a large family in Columbus, Ohio, and have spent most of my life as a self-employed digital nomad of sorts. Writing has been a favorite pastime of mine for many years now, and I've been enjoying this hobby on the internet since the age of twelve, the age when I began my first blog on Xanga.com.

Most of my life has felt like a journey from one place to another: living, working, and traveling across the globe in my now thirty-three years of age. I lost my Dad to cancer at the age of twenty. That hurt a lot. It also made me question whether or not I, too, wanted to be a Father someday.

I wrestled (a lot) with the idea of parenting. I didn't want to start a family that I would have to one day say goodbye to, regardless of the joy that would inevitably come from having a child. Being a Dad is one of the highest callings one can embark upon. It's a lifetime full of sacrifice, work, patience, and time given to your loved ones, ahead of yourself.

As I grew older, I realized many of my treasured memories come from moments when my Dad took time out of his busy schedule to spend it with me and make me feel important. Even a thirty-three-year-old man melts when he thinks about the times his Dad threw him into the pool or took him for rides in his 1977 Land Cruiser.

Dads are important. Their role goes far beyond raising and providing for their families; it extends to the preparation, grooming, and training of the next generation of men and women in the world, who will someday have families of their own.

Who is this book for? It's for many people, really. It's for the young man who just found out his partner is pregnant and is struggling to find peace—very much like my own journey. It's for the children whose parent or parents walked out on them before they were old enough to remember what they looked like. It's for the parents who want to provide their children with words of encouragement, love, and kindness, even if they don't know how to say or write them.

This book is for the people questioning (like I did) whether or not they are fit to be good parents during these crazy times in the world (you are).

In the months of preparation for being a Dad, I spent countless hours on the internet, looking for testimonials from expectant Dads so I could learn the struggle they faced as they came closer to fatherhood. Often, I found encouragement in the testimonials, which offered their authentic fears, concerns, and thoughts freely to the camera—and to anybody who would listen. I was one of those people.

When I was twenty years old, I woke up to a phone call from my Mom, letting me know my Dad had finally surrendered in his fight with colon cancer. Ever since that day, my life hasn't been the same as I've struggled to navigate this plane[t] without the guidance and love that only a Dad can offer his children. It's been hard. However, the years have also had their share of joy, accomplishment, laughter and love.

Similar to my own Opa (Grandfather), who wrote a book about his life, I now drop these pages into the proverbial pond of time. I don't know how far the ripples will carry or who will find encouragement in them. However, it was never my job to know the outcome of *Dear Atlas*. It was simply my job to write the notes, pour my heart out to little Atlas ahead of his birth, and share any wisdom or experiences I've acquired in my thirty-three years of life.

> *Dear Atlas*
> *Someday you will be reading these letters*
> *Long beyond the days when I am with you*
> *When I am gone, do not worry, do not despair*
> *My last breath with you will give birth to far more*
> *Sometime, someplace, somewhere*
> *I will be there*
>
> *Do not look for me in your sadness*
> *I will not be there*
> *Do not try to find me in your pain*
> *I won't be there either*

Look for me in the sunrise that greets each day
Listen for my voice in the sound of birds
Feel my spirit when you surrender to the forest trails
Look for me in distant ocean waves and gusty breezes of air
That's where you will find me—as you find yourself.

Love,
Dad

March 1: The Beginning

Dear Atlas,

It's me, your Dad.

Right now, you only know me through the sound of my voice, which you hear from the muffled insulation of the womb. You're still inside your Mom right now!

I realized it's never too early for me to start writing to you, to let you know how excited I am to be your Dad—and to share with you the love I have for you, your Mom, and our growing family.

I don't know what the world will be like when you're finally reading these letters. At the rate it's going now, I imagine it will be pretty interesting. 2020 was a very strange year for many. Yet, it was also the year when we found out you were coming.

I wish I could write that I feel prepared for your arrival, or that your Mom and I carefully planned the moment when you came into this world. However, that's not the way things went—or how life tends to go.

The story of you has been an interesting journey filled with plane rides, international border crossings, and a roller coaster of a relationship that sparked the love between your Mom and me.

How I met your Mom is a helluva story. I was living in Ohio, she in California. One evening I got a message from a mutual friend of ours, which read:

"Have you ever met her? I think you two would make a great couple."

Atlas, that was how things started. Something happened when I read that note: I felt like I was ready to be the other half of a couple. It's hard to explain, but for most of my dating life, I never really saw the "couple" dynamic as much as I saw two individuals who sniffed each other's butts for a few months at a time before moving on their way, just like dogs do at a park.

A couple. What did that mean? I saw it as *finally becoming* a two-person unit that did things together, like live in one home, cook meals, and wake up on rainy Tuesday mornings and see each other. I saw it as finally meeting somebody who would hear me fart, see me cry, and accept the parts of me that I didn't feel were good enough to offer . . . anybody.

I'll have you know that I've wondered whether or not I wanted to have a family for many years now. My heart knew I wanted a family, but my head was busy trying to talk me out of it. You'll understand the head/heart battle when you get older, Atlas.

Well, your Mom and I met in California. I flew to Los Angeles to watch her run a marathon (oddly enough, I had a dream I was running one last night) and we drove back to San Francisco together, where I moved into a small room in a shared house.

Your Mom had her own apartment, which was full of her family: her Mom and Dad, two cats, and a dog (Brindley!).

I won't ever forget how your Mom and I had one date night in San Francisco before the city shut down due to the pandemic. You'll understand that when you get older, too.

Those few months of being shut in were really difficult. We'd meet in public parks, take long walks, and sit by the ocean while drinking five-dollar to-go margaritas, eating Mexican food, and giving our scraps to the hordes of birds that buzzed around us.

One day your Mom suggested we take a trip and mentioned Tulum. Admittedly, I didn't know anything about Tulum, other than hearing it tossed around as a trip idea by an old friend of mine. So, we went.

At the time, I think we were both ready to escape San Francisco and what it had become: closed-off, dying, and suspicious. The city we had both fallen in love with was no longer what we remembered it to be. So, we packed our bags and prepared to go to Mexico for a month-long vacation.

Those thirty days turned into much more than that. It's now March 1 . . . and we went to Mexico last June.

I wish I could tell you that our relationship was perfect and without fights. However, that wouldn't be truthful. Your Mom and I had an uphill battle getting along. When things were good, they were *great*. But when things were bad, Atlas . . . they were horrible, and we both did many things we are now ashamed of.

Yet, we persisted, Atlas. We kept showing up for each other, offering apologies when needed, and taking time to learn from the mistakes we made with each other.

The more time we spent together, the more I came to realize that your Mom was exactly the kind of woman I hoped to meet, marry, and have a family with. Is she wild and crazy? Yes. But so is her heart, and I fell head-over-heels in love with a woman who loved me more fiercely than any other I've met before.

That's something I want you to know about your Mom: she is the fiercest Mama Bear you will ever meet.

She is strong, capable, intelligent, protective, and gorgeous.

Atlas, as your Dad, I want you to know that I want you to be here. Not just with your Mom and me, but here on this plane[t].

The world is going a little crazy right now, and it's desperately in need of good people, which is who your Mom and I hope to raise you to be.

We don't care if you grow up to become rich, famous, or even poor. What we want most for you (and I'm speaking on behalf of us both right now, since your Mom is asleep in the bedroom with you) is to live from the heart. We want you to be somebody who lives a full life; loves others; and gives life to their ideas, passions, and interests.

We hope you will be a fun, creative, and kind young man who is respectful of others, gives to the poor, and knows how to be a good listener.

We're both committed to creating an environment for you where you will be able to succeed, grow, and feel supported by both of your parents.

As your Dad, I want you to know I'm here for you and always will be. I hope you grow up having the experience of knowing me personally, not just through my writing, but through quality time shared together. I hope I can set an example for you of what it means to be a good person, Dad, husband, and human being. I hope your Mom and I set an example for you of how to have a loving relationship that goes the distance.

More than anything, we both hope you grow up feeling loved in your head and your heart.

In six weeks, you'll be here with us, and we couldn't be happier.

Until then, kiddo, I love you and I am so proud to be your Dad.

Love,
Dad

March 2

Dear Atlas,

It's me, your Dad.

Today is a really big day for your Mom and me. It's the day when we get to see you. Yes, you! Your Mom scheduled a 4D ultrasound (cover your ears, kiddo!) so we can see you one last time before we hold you in our arms.

If there's one thing you ought to know about your Dad, it's that I have a lot of anticipation for things that are on the way, whether it's you, an important date, a package in the mail, or a life event. For better or for worse, I've always kept one eye looking ahead at the future and wondered what it would bring.

I feel that way about you, Son. I wonder what life will be like when you finally arrive. There are a lot of questions going through my mind since I'm your Dad.

Someday, you may find yourself asking yourself these questions, too:

What will he look like?

Will he cry a lot?

Will his Mom and I be able to work as a team?

How bad will his diapers smell?

Will we get any sleep?

Will we have a comfortable life?

What will his personality be like?

When will he take his first step?

When will he be born?

How much will he weigh?

Will I be a good Dad? Husband? Role model?

All of these questions are going through my mind right now, Atlas. As your Dad, I've sometimes felt a bit lost as I see these questions racing through my mind.

That's when I think back to my own upbringing. How did my parents do? Well, they did a mighty fine job, Son. No, things weren't always perfect. But I had one of the best childhoods I could have imagined.

I suppose you know you had a healthy childhood when you can look back at all of the memories with appreciation instead of trying to block them out (consciously or unconsciously).

My parents did a great job raising their family, the ones you will now know as uncles and aunts, and an Oma.

Even as we prepare to see you today, I have a wave of peace knowing that you're here—already. You aren't an idea or a "what if" statement; you're in our house now, even as I write this. That brings me a lot of joy, Atlas.

You should see your Mom, too. She's the most beautiful I've ever seen her. You'll understand someday if you ever find yourself with a pregnant partner. It's like the sun came down and touched her body with its rays, illuminating her from the inside out with you.

I won't make things weird for you . . . but you should know that your Mom is a babe. And even more so since she became pregnant with you.

You'll find out when you're older.

There are a lot of things you'll find out when you're older. But I want you to know that where you are now, and where you will always be in each moment, is exactly where you need to be. I hope you grow up with an appreciation for each moment, without being too concerned about the next, because the next moment always comes—just like each sunrise in the morning.

While we are counting down the days until you arrive, we're also enjoying each moment we have before you get here: soaking in the quiet time, drinking in each second we have with each other (and each other), and preparing ourselves for the moment you arrive.

Atlas, if there's one thing I could have told myself many years ago about having a family, and that I would like you to know when the time comes for you to have a family, it's this:

When you're ready to have a family, the time will present itself. I promise you, you will never feel ready, because that simply isn't possible. However, God knows when you are ready and will make the moment happen when you are ripe for the picking.

Don't be afraid, either. There's so much more to look forward to in the joy of having a family than in anything you will miss from being a bachelor. Trust me—you won't miss anything more than the joy you experience when you see your own son for the first time, staring up at you with eyes that see a loving father, provider, husband, and guardian.

Yes, you will be a guardian. And it's a huge responsibility to bring a life into this world, more so than anything you've ever done. You're fit for the job, and you've been preparing for this moment since you were in diapers.

Trust God. Love your partner. Be good to yourself. And, most importantly, surrender to each moment and receive all of the surprises it contains.

Life happens when you least expect it.

See you soon, Atlas.

Love,
Dad

March 3: Your Face

Dear Atlas,

It's me, your Dad.

Yesterday was an incredible day for your Mom and me. We got to see your face! Well, part of it. Your hands seem to have gotten in the way . . .

Your Mom and I went for a 4D ultrasound, where we were able to see a few parts of your body in 3D, namely, your hands, eyes, lips . . . and genitals. You're definitely a little boy!

Seeing you on the ultrasound has been a really special part of the pregnancy. For me, especially. It's helped me to develop the growing emotional connection to you that occurs between child and Father.

I'll admit it's been really hard for me throughout the pregnancy, because I don't *feel* a strong connection with you, like your Mom does. She's the one carrying you, and able to feel every kick, push, and flutter you make inside of her.

You should see the way she loves you, Atlas. Even before you are born, she's absolutely wild about you.

One of my favorite memories of her involved walking into our bedroom and finding her with a huge smile on her face.

"What's going on?" I asked.

"Atlas is ticklish!" she said, and proceeded to tickle the side of her belly, which triggered little movements from you.

Even though she and I have different emotional connections with you (and I think we always will, and are supposed to), the one thing we share is the memories we have during this pregnancy.

We have laughed, loved, traveled the world, and shared our hopes, fears, dreams, and thoughts with each other—with you sandwiched between us in all of these things.

Last night we talked about the connection we'll share when you're an infant. I mentioned to your Mom that I felt it would be hard to connect with you as an infant and that I didn't know how, as your Dad, to give you the things you'd need.

"You can change his diapers, help feed him, hold him, and give him love," she said.

These things aren't the native parts of being a Dad that came to mind for me. Yet, she's right; a big portion of your life involves this sort of love, and it will come long ahead of the times when you and I will have our Father-Son adventures; taking trips to the store, cooking breakfast for your Mom, going on hikes, playing in the ocean, or learning how to change the oil in our cars.

Sometimes I get ahead of myself, Atlas. And I find myself yearning for things that aren't quite ready yet—just like you! You're still growing, developing, and putting on weight as you prepare to come into this world.

In so many ways, your Mom and I are also growing a lot during this last trimester. We're learning how to communicate better, how to respect each other, and, most importantly, how to accept each other as we are without trying to change the other.

As your Dad, that's my hope for you: that you'll be raised in an environment where you feel empowered to be yourself and supported by both of your parents no matter what direction you choose to go.

We don't know what you'll be like, Atlas. We both wonder what your personality will be like, how you'll look, what kind of food you'll like (or spit out), and what you'll do as a young adult.

That's part of the beauty that's you: you're a little bit of both of us, but we've combined to create **you**, a perfect little human being deserving of love, attention, care, respect, and infinite amounts of cuddling.

Yesterday wasn't the day to see your face. But I'm okay with that. Soon you will be resting in our arms, and we'll be able to see you for the beautiful miracle that you are . . . and change your diapers.

I love you,
Dad

March 4

Dear Atlas,

It's me, your Dad.

Time seems to be moving at a million miles an hour, while standing still at the same time. It feels this way because you are coming. Soon.

Usually, moments of finality are accompanied by unpleasant things. However, that's not the case with you. I feel a tremendous amount of excitement for the day you arrive, and for all that will follow as our family dynamic comes to life.

It's a complex emotion, though. And I wish somebody had given me a better explanation of what to expect as I prepare for your birth and take on the responsibility of being a Dad. Since nobody gave me "the talk," I hope I can impart some of my experience to you years before you ever have a family of your own.

When somebody asks me if I'm excited about your birth, there's always a slight pause before I give an affirmative answer. Why the pause? Because I see the infinite number of things that come along with your birth.

Having a child isn't the same as buying a house or a car. However, I think a house is a good example to use.

A new homeowner is incredibly excited to walk into their new house. However, they also have a realization that behind the doors of their house is the responsibility to maintain, furnish, appreciate, and live in the house. It suddenly becomes a very real part of their life experience with a sense of finality they probably didn't have while they rented.

You look at the house and begin to wonder about all of the memories that will occur inside of it: eating a family dinner, inviting guests over, experiencing the inevitable fights/disagreements and the simple joys that come with occupying a space with somebody you love.

You know, things like cooking together, having coffee in the mornings, relaxing after a long day, being there to watch your partner say "Ahhh" when they take their bra off after a long day (and the joy that comes with that moment as a man . . .).

I digress. Back to you, Atlas.

There's a lot that comes with you entering our lives, and I've never, ever felt the way I do now as I prepare for your arrival in my mind, body, and spirit. I see you being a tremendous participant in our family's happiness—not the source, because that's a lot of pressure to put on a child.

Rather, I want you to know that you are an integral part of our family. After all, the word *family* wouldn't really be the case if you weren't a part of it. Rather, your Mom and I would be a couple, as many people are who don't have children.

I used to think having a child would only be a lot of work or responsibility. So, the notion of having a family really worried me because I didn't associate it with the joy and memories that also came with having a child.

Honestly, kiddo, it seemed like nothing more than a burden and something to be terrified of.

I'll tell you when that moment changed for me, because I think you ought to know.

One evening, your Mom and I were going to dinner at one of our favorite places in Tulum (we live there, by the way!) and she mentioned she had a surprise for me.

It had been a very long day for me, and I didn't know what sort of surprise she had in store. Would it be a gift? A back massage? A new pair of underwear? Yes, these were my initial thoughts . . . you'll understand someday.

Instead, she pulled out a small piece of paper with an intricate symbol drawn in black marker on the back of it. She slid it across the table, and I began to read the note by the light of the candle.

Someday, you'll read the note, which has gone through many evolutions and repairs.

It was the announcement of your gender.

Here's a paraphrase since I don't have the note in front of me: ". . . two pairs of Plaat footsteps walking in the sand . . . Father and Son."

"We're going to have a boy!" I said, looking up from the paper. Instantly, a wave of emotion hit me, and I began to shed tears of joy.

A son! You! Another Plaat!

The moment was incredibly special, Atlas. We couldn't contain our emotion as the waiter came to the table, seeing the excitement and tears in our eyes. We shared with him that we were having a son, and he offered his congratulations—and even gave me a hug, right on the spot!

A hug from a stranger during the pandemic was a rare treat.

That moment, Atlas, was the moment when all of my worries about having a family were met with the joys that would inevitably come with you. I wish I had an answer for why they didn't come until that point. However, I don't.

Timing is an incredible thing. And, in our case, I'm glad all of the anticipation and joy waited its turn before showing up.

The story of you has been an incredible one, Son. I'd venture to say it's more like a miracle than a traditional birth story.

Every child is special, Atlas. But I think you are especially special—after all, our taxi driver called you "*El futuro de Tulum.*"

The future of Tulum.

I love you, Atlas. Your Mom does, too.

Te veo pronto, hijo.

Dad

March 5

Dear Atlas,

It's me, your Dad.

You've been popping up in my dreams a lot. For the past few nights, I've had dreams where I'm conscious you are coming, and had many conversations with the people I encounter in the dreams about how I feel as I prepare to be a father.

I wish I could tell you I feel ready to be your Dad, but that wouldn't be entirely true. From what I've heard (and experienced), there isn't anything that will ever make someone feel ready to be a parent, and that doesn't make anyone a bad person.

When I look around, I see a lot of people who seem to really nail the parenting thing. Diaper-bag-toting parent warriors who can change a dirty diaper, prepare a snack, and clean up a mess in three seconds flat, or parents who seem to have an "everything bag" that never runs out of the supplies required for a day trip.

You'll understand the struggle a lot more when you get older. Hopefully I'll be able to share some of my learnings with you and help you prepare for the role of being a Dad, Partner, and Man, three things that most people seem to struggle with in this day and age.

Love,
Dad

March 6

Dear Atlas,

It's me, your Dad.

Time feels like it's flying by and standing still at the same time. I can't say you'll understand this feeling when you get older, because you might not. I certainly didn't expect to feel this way.

I'm eager to hold you in my arms and connect the dots of your arrival with what that means for us as a family.

Things haven't quite been the same since I found out you were coming into our lives. There was a finality that didn't exist in my mind before, the knowledge that you would soon be a living, breathing human being and nothing will ever change that.

I'm thirty-three, Atlas. And I've had a really wonderful life—and continue to. If there's one thing I've learned in life, it's that it *really does* get better over time. Not for everybody, but for the people who see the sunrise each day and greet it with a smile.

That's easier said than done, Son. It's also a lot easier to do than you might think. When I start my morning with gratitude, things seem to go a lot better that day. However, when I start the day off with stress and worry, it tanks the day.

These days, you're one of the first things I see in the morning, along with your beautiful Mom. In the background, I see a beautiful jungle full of birds and fresh morning air. I can't help but feel like I'm a participant in the most wonderful life I ever could have asked for—and I get to share it with you and your Mom.

That, my Son, is worth everything.

I love you,
Dad

March 7

Dear Atlas,

It's me, your Dad.

Ahead of your birth, I've started to see things differently; it feels like my perspective is widening and I'm understanding things with a new depth, a new dimension. One of those things is how I communicate with you, and with your Mom.

I think a lot about how you and I will communicate, whether that's in the way of me holding you as an infant and looking into your eyes or if it's through the talks we will inevitably have as you mature and grow older.

I hope we can communicate a position of stability, Atlas. I also hope you know it's okay to be yourself, as you are. Your Great-Opa (great-grandfather) wrote a book about his life that reflected, in great length and detail, his journey as a child.

He faced many challenges and opponents simply for being himself. And he felt that harsh judgment his entire life. He said he wished somebody had gone back and told that little boy that it was okay, and that he was a perfectly fine young man as he was, would be, and will be.

Because he didn't experience somebody telling him so directly, he went on to chase the answer in many different ways. He fought, ran, flew, and raced his way through a life that was nonstop adventure . . . and risk.

He was lucky to have made it through his life relatively unscarred. At least, on the outside.

I think he was really asking "Do you love me? Am I good enough? Are you proud of me?" with all of his actions and choices. Perhaps he was asking those questions of his father, or himself, or his lover.

As a man, you'll find yourself asking those questions a lot, Atlas. They never quite seem to find a permanent answer if we don't let them. I still ask these questions, Son—a lot, knowing you're on the way.

Now is a moment when I'm doing my best to take the advice I now write to you, Atlas, the knowledge that you are more than enough and perfectly okay as you are.

Love,

Dad

March 8

Dear Atlas,

It's me, your Dad.

I often wonder what sights, sounds, and experiences you will encounter during your life. Knowing your Mom and me, I imagine you'll have a pretty vibrant life experience.

I'm still getting used to the idea of you being here soon. The part of me that is excited for your arrival doesn't seem to be firmly cemented in place because there are moments when your arrival feels far from my mind.

The thought of you coming brings me a lot of joy, Atlas. Joy, if we're able to get it right together as your parents—and as individuals.

It didn't take a lot of planning to create you, Son. One thing led to another, and the next thing we both knew, we were looking at a positive pregnancy test. That was the startling thing: it came so easily.

The real planning and work come as we think about what it takes to raise a family. I think the word *raise* is important here, because there's a level of consciousness-raising that occurs in a relationship, the one that leads to a family.

That's the part that isn't fun: when you see the parts of yourself that need to change, evolve, adapt, or be eliminated.

I'm fighting that right now, Atlas. I won't make any excuses about it; I'm feeling resistance to making changes (even the necessary ones) and discovering what's around the corner.

You're worth it, Atlas. We all are.

Love,
Dad

March 9

Dear Atlas,

It's me, your Dad.

There's something special about your letter this morning. I'm writing it while listening to some music my Dad loved (Steve Taylor, *Liver*, track 7 . . . if you're ever curious), and it feels like time has stopped as our generations are connecting to each other.

My Dad taught me a lot of lessons, Atlas. Some lessons he taught by example; other times, he taught with his words, choices, or discipline. I hated being on the receiving end of the last one.

Expecting you, I think a lot about the way you and I will develop our relationship. I'm a bit beyond the opinion that it's my sole job to teach you the ways of the world. Rather, I think it's my job to do that for myself and live an example that would serve you well if you chose to follow it, all of it or in part. You may find even greater benefit for your life by choosing to do some things differently. That's all up to you.

My favorite moments with my own Dad were the times he chose to spend only with me. I felt like I was on the receiving end of his full attention, and it felt cool to do things with a man I looked up to, who towered like a giant over many other adults.

The biggest man in the room was my own Dad. I loved that. You might like it, too. I hope you do. And I don't mean you'll love seeing me be the biggest human in the room, but the one who appears most alive, authentic, and honest to you—my Son.

One of my lessons in life came from trying to be this version to others, before choosing to be it myself—to myself.

That's one of those lessons you don't really learn until you learn it. It took me thirty-three years, and I'm still discovering the need to accept myself fully and to be good to myself.

Already, you've taught me a lot, Son. I want you to know that. I hope the lessons never stop coming from you, too.

Life will be a lot better with you in it, Atlas. My life. Her life. Our life. Your life. Us.

Keep growing strong. You'll come when you're ready.

Love,
Dad

March 10

Dear Atlas,

It's me, your Dad.

It's another beautiful morning: writing to you, listening to Steve Taylor (*Squint*, track 3), and thinking of your arrival.

Your Mom and I keep having dreams about you. I dreamed about you last night. You're a beautiful baby, and it was amazing to see both of us in *you*. I certainly can't wait to hold you in my arms and do everything possible to create an environment of love for our family.

Your arrival has certainly been an abrupt event. Your Mom and I are both highly independent people who probably planned on having children "one day," but didn't seem to have it on our radar that a positive pregnancy test would come so soon.

In a lot of ways, anticipating you has brought about a lot of positive change. Your Mom and I are connecting in new ways (and letting go of old ones) and have a shared common goal of *us*, our family.

You're part of that, Atlas. A really big part. We see the opportunity we have to provide you with a great life, one that will be meaningful, rich, and full of wonderful memories with your parents. Experiences, trips, meals together, conversation, the ever-fun day trips to the grocery store, and whatever other adventures we find ourselves in.

I know one of the best things I can do for our family is to be a man of my word. It's easy to make promises, but difficult to fulfill them. Even if it's something small (like writing to you every day), I'm doing my best to be better at keeping my commitments, promises, and goals intact.

I love you, Atlas.
Dad

March 11

Dear Atlas,

It's me, your Dad.

When you get older, you'll recognize an hourglass on my right arm. Someday you'll be old enough to understand the story, and the legacy, behind it.

As you get older, you'll realize you are a part of that legacy. It's a legacy that includes the story of your parents: who they were before they met and who they became after.

I'm watching an hourglass right now, Atlas. Each second that passes delivers a small trickle of sand. It reminds me a lot of the life we have. Some moments, I feel like I'm trying to push the sand through the hole to make it go faster. Other times, I'm grasping at grains of sand that are slipping through my fingers.

That's how I know I have a wonderful life, Atlas: I see the mix of times I wish could go faster paired with moments I don't want to let go of. I'm right there in the middle, with your Mom—and with you.

I'm really thankful for you, Atlas. I want you to know that. I'm thankful because you've brought welcome change into my life. Somehow it makes things more real, knowing you're on the way.

I take things more seriously now because I see that everything has a response. Whether that's an action, word, or moment, the things we do matter.

I see the hourglass draining, and I'm filled with gratitude because I know the moments I've lived up until this point have been wonderful. And there are so many new moments of wonder, joy, laughter, and love ahead now that you're on the horizon.

I can't wait to see you and dance with you in the mornings.

Love,
Dad

March 12

Dear Atlas,

It's me, your Dad.

Every time I look at the date stamp on these entries, I do a quick countdown of the days we have before you arrive.

You're coming quickly, Atlas. We're both ready for you and excited for you to finally arrive.

For most of my life, I worried about what this time would look like when it arrived. Pregnancy, that is. I wondered what sort of environment I would be in when I heard the words "I'm pregnant," as well as what the state of my own affairs would be when or if it finally happened.

I set some goals in my mind for what I'd need in order to have a child and feel good about it. I thought I'd need to have a certain amount of income or money in the bank. Properties, cars, multiple streams of income . . . the list grew.

Now that you're on the way, I wonder if all of those must-haves were really just parts of myself that I needed to overcome the "need" for—not just before having a family, but also to improve myself as a human being. All of those things come and go. Love is what remains and matters.

If I could go back and tell myself one thing during all those moments I questioned, it'd be this:

"Aaron, when the moment comes for you to have a family, you will be perfectly equipped with all the tools you need for the job.

—Me

P.S. Those things are not the ones you think you need."

P.P.S. —Dad

March 13

Dear Atlas,

It's me, your Dad.

Your Mom and I are having one of those days, the kind I hope you get to experience in your life: priceless moments, laughter, connection, and true intimacy.

We both want a lot of wonderful things for you, Atlas. We're going to do our very best to create an environment where you can thrive—as your own person.

It's starting to really sink in that you could arrive in our lives at any moment now. Stranger things have happened. However, I do hope you come as planned and arrive in your best health.

I really can't wait to hold you. I'm going to fall in love with you as soon as I see you . . . I just know it.

See you soon,

Dad

March 15

Dear Atlas,

It's me, your Dad.

I wanted to let you know that I didn't forget about writing to you yesterday. Your Mom and I gave each other our one-hundred-percent attention yesterday, and that meant "us" time. You'll understand when you get older.

It's becoming very real to me (and to your Mom) that you will be here any day now. That thought still triggers a big exclamation point in my energy, a lot of excitement, joy, uncertainty, and admittedly—fear.

Whenever the fear arises, I try to remember that nothing in life would ever make me feel one hundred percent ready to be a parent. Yet, when I look at you, and at and my own life, I realize how ready I am to be a Dad.

"With every baby comes a loaf of bread" is a saying I once heard. Whenever I hear that, I think about the wonderful blessings that will occur once you are born.

I think about memories I haven't had yet but I know are certain to come because of you being in our lives: sharing laughter, enjoying breakfasts together, writing notes for your Mom, rocking you to sleep, and making eye contact for the first time.

When I was younger, I didn't have the consciousness or capacity for these ideas. I think that's why I feared having a family. Now that you're on the way, all of these revelations have come to me, and I now feel an excitement for you that I didn't know I could have ahead of your birth.

I'm ready for you, Atlas. And I want you to be here.

Love,
Dad

March 18

Dear Atlas,

It's me, your Dad.

While you didn't get a note from me yesterday, I think you got something better: a day together with me and your Mom, shopping for you!

Part of getting ready for you is buying you things. A lot of things. It seems like there are a lot of must-have accessories, tools, and secret items that only moms know about, and that they only find out about shortly before they have a child.

I'll admit it felt somewhat strange to walk through the baby aisles as a shopper, as somebody intent on making purchases in those aisles. Normally, my only walk through the "Infants & Toddlers" section comes as part of a shortcut to another section of the store.

It's starting to sink in that you're on the way, for this reason among many. I don't yet feel like a Dad, Atlas. However, I don't feel like a non-Dad, either.

This transformation can feel a little overwhelming at times, Atlas. It's as if you're exchanging one outfit for another at the same time. Some parts of me are growing, while other parts are being worked out of my system because they no longer serve me.

It feels like another version of going through puberty, only as an adult.

Your Dad has to work now but loves you very much and is thinking about you.

Keep growing, Atlas. Give your Mom a break today, please. She's pooped.

Love,
Dad

March 19

Dear Atlas,

It's me, your Dad.

Time feels like it's racing by as your Mom and I prepare for your arrival. We both have a long list of things we need to accomplish before you arrive.

We're excited for you, Atlas. I'm excited for you.

I feel a lot of things changing in my life, and in my mind. I no longer feel "me-centric," focused on myself. Now, I think about the well-being of your Mom and you.

I wish more kids knew they were loved, appreciated, and wanted before they arrived, Atlas. I've met a lot of people who feel like they don't have a seat at the table in life.

I've wondered if its due to them not knowing they were wanted.

You are wanted, Atlas. And you have been since before you were born.

I love you,
Dad

March 20

Dear Atlas,

It's me, your Dad.

Time seems like it's flying by, and I can't help but get more excited about all the moments we will share as a family.

For many years, I fought the idea of having a family. Coming from a large one, I sometimes questioned whether a family was the solution I was looking for in my life.

I feared a loss of independence, and of . . . me-ness, as if somehow, I'd come up short every day if I had children.

Now that you're on the way, I realize I had it all wrong. I'm not losing something in myself, but gaining something incredible with you, your Mom, and the "us" that will be our family. Us.

One of my own fears is being alone, Atlas. I think many other people feel that way, too. My own fear of being alone comes from the belief that I have something to offer somebody and want to receive something from another. That idea is also at the root of having a family; I truly believe I have something to offer you with my life, time, and love.

Tools for the job, Atlas. I hope that's what I can offer you: examples, lessons, and conversations to help you shape your own life. My Dad gave me tools to create my own life, Atlas.

For years, I've lived, worked, and existed from my heart (though my head was sometimes far up where the sun don't shine), and it's largely been because I've had lessons—and tools—passed down to me from those I love. Especially from my Dad.

Dads have a special connection with their children. However, there's something particularly special about the connection a Father has with his Son. This connection is something I'm excited to share with you.

Just so you know, this doesn't mean I dream of doing only "manly" things with you or that I even have gender-specific boxes for activities. What I look forward to sharing is a mutual understanding of what it means to be a man, as a man. In this way, I hope I'll be able to help you understand the world and never feel alone or misunderstood.

Today's another special day for you, for us: we're having a photo shoot together, as a family.

I can't wait to show you the pictures and read these notes to you. Somewhere, someday.

I love you,
Dad

March 21

Dear Atlas,

It's me, your Dad.

The clock continues to tick until your arrival. Every day seems to bring something new with it as I think about what it means to have a family.

Family comes in many shapes and sizes, Atlas. In some cases, people find it with people other than the ones they grew up with. Other times, that birth family connection remains intact—and familiar—for most of their lives.

I already know our family won't be a traditional one, Atlas. Your Mom and I are far too much "ourselves" to give you a vanilla life, though that's what you might want to have someday—which is fine. Ultimately, I think we will both feel like we succeeded with you when you discover what you want and go for it, even if it's unique or different from the environment we have as a family.

I'm on a journey right now, in many ways. I'm preparing for you in my head, heart, soul, and hands. Your Mom will soon give birth to you, and I feel something is being born (and created) from inside of me as well.

What's happening right now is that your Mom and I are finding new ways to live as we prepare for you. New ways to get along with each other, but also ways to welcome you into the home where you will be raised.

We're each on our own journey, Atlas. You are, too! That's the beauty I find in all of this: all three of us are growing, stretching, and experiencing new life at the same time, as a family.

We couldn't do this without you, Atlas.

I love you,
Dad

March 22

Dear Atlas,

It's me, your Dad.

I think a lot about the type of person you're going to be. Your Mom and I are really curious to see what your personality is like, what foods you'll like, and what you'll look like. All of these questions will be answered in time, like a lot of the questions I'm carrying inside my head before you arrive. I wonder what things will be like for me as your Dad.

Dad is a special role that I don't think gets nearly enough credit. In a world where everybody wants their turn in the "discrimination awareness" spotlight, Dads seem to be so far behind, they don't even try to make an appearance. More often than not, the Dad is portrayed as a buffoon in TV shows and Hollywood movies.

I would hate for you to spend your whole life with a feeling that your major lot in life is to be the butt of jokes made by your own family. Truth is, Atlas, the role of the Dad is a silent journey. I don't think most men want accolades, or even recognition, for what they do, at least not as much as the time and space to do it their own way.

I think what I feel most right now is the desire to get things right with you, your Mom, and my own life. It's difficult for me to feel that way right now, Atlas. Ahead of you being born, I feel like I'm not doing nearly enough in life.

What I do know is that there's a lot of support in our corner, little guy. Your Mom is incredible, and I know we will be able to work as a family in all that we do: the highs, lows, and everything in between.

I love you,
Dad

March 23

Dear Atlas,

It's me, your Dad.

Lately, life feels like it's going in fast-forward and rewind at the same time. By the time you read this, you won't understand where the term "rewind" came from.

However, you'll know things then that I don't know now. We'll have shared many memories as a family.

Sometimes when I sit down to write to you, the words come easily to me; it feels like I had something specific to tell you that day, which found its relief when the words found their way to the screen.

Other days, I sit down and have a hard time putting together my thoughts. This morning, I realized the simple act of writing to you—consistently—is one of the first of many ways I'll tell you I love you.

I had a hard time with my own Dad because he'd often make promises to me that he wasn't able to deliver on. I say he "wasn't able to" instead of he "broke his promises" because as I get older, I realize what it means to have bandwidth—and how it can run in short supply, despite the best of intentions.

When I first sat down to write to you, I made a note that I would do so every day. It was one of my own stress tests for being a Dad; I wanted to have something I could begin committing to in the relationship you and I will have.

Well, Atlas, I have to start some other commitments. Part of my commitment to being a good Dad for you involves providing for our family. Deadlines are due today.

I love you, kiddo.
Dad

March 24

Dear Atlas,

It's me, your Dad.

By the time you read this, I don't know what it will be like in the world, either mine or yours. I know our future together will be filled with memories, laughter, and love as a family.

Family is the greatest treasure you can have, Atlas. That's a lesson you'll find out someday. If I had to explain this lesson to you in a way that you'd understand as time went by, it would go something like this:

When you stub your toe on the side of a couch (or on the very sharp edge of a live wood slab on our coffee table . . .), the only thing you can think about is pain. Nothing else matters at that moment. Trust me, you aren't thinking about the bills that are due or the last time you laughed, made love, or cried. You're in a moment of excruciating pain.

Family is the inverse of that. They are the common thread of love that you can rely on for support in your life.

It doesn't come easily, though. Your Mom and I will be the first to tell you that our relationship took some fine-tuning, a few phone calls and some heartfelt conversations with each other . . . while the bags were packed.

Through it all, I've learned to love your Mom—and you—a lot more. Our conflicts were a lot like the stubbed-toe scenario. One of us "stubbed" an emotional toe (our own or the other's) and a reaction ensued that blinded us to everything else.

We chose to stay, Atlas. We held our ground, drew our boundaries, and learned to love, respect, and forgive each other in new dimensions.

A lot can happen in a short time; nothing reminds me of this universal truth more than you. You're growing every single day. There is nothing in the universe more complex, valuable, or intricate than . . . you.

I love you, Atlas. You aren't a tiny speck in the universe, but an entirely new universe in a human-sized package.

Love,

Dad

March 25

Dear Atlas,

It's me, your Dad.

Your arrival is so close, it nearly feels like you're here already. But the time with your Mom has been dear and sweet as we prepare for you.

I've started to see your Mom differently since you were conceived. As you've grown inside of her, she has blossomed in her beauty, care, and radiance. You should see her, Atlas. She's beautiful.

Through your pregnancy, I've started to see myself differently as well. Whenever I look back at my relationship with my own Father, I think of the times that went well, and of those I wish could have gone differently. That's where you come into the picture. Now it's up to me to do things differently and be that change for you (and for myself) as your Dad and as a husband to your Mom.

Things don't get done on their own, Atlas. Time is the most valuable commodity you have. I hope we get to spend a lot of it together as a family.

I want to be happy, healthy, and well for our family, Atlas. I want that first for myself because it has to start from me. Lately I've been paying attention to my own habits (good and bad) and have started to see how much everything I do will impact a larger circle than me: us, our family.

That revelation brings me a new perspective, as well as a desire to live a healthy life together as a family.

I can't wait to look into those beautiful eyes of yours.

You are precious, irreplaceable, wonderful, and loved!

Love,
Dad

March 26

Dear Atlas,

It's me, your Dad.

We're in the final countdown until your birth, and each day that passes feels special as your Mom and I take the final steps toward meeting you.

You, Atlas. I've been thinking about you a lot. No matter where I find myself in the day, you're somewhere in my thoughts. I wonder what you'll be like. I catch glimpses of memories that haven't happened yet. I also think of the times we'll be bonding as a family. There are many wonderful memories ahead.

I've learned a lot about myself in this process, Atlas. Ever since you were conceived, I've felt my own countdown to sort things out in my life. Some things need to change. Other things need to stay.

Most of all, I need to take accountability for my actions in a greater way than I have before.

Yesterday I was doing the dishes and a thought hit me: "There are many ways to say 'I love you.'" And that can include a variety of things—doing the dishes, for example.

Your Mom has loved me in new ways lately, too. It's as if a new dimension is opening up between us, the "us" part that needs to work as a team. That "us" is a powerful thing, Atlas. You can count on it when you need encouragement, and it will never let you down. However, you have to give yourself to it fully if you want to reap those benefits.

I'm trying my best not to want or wish you to be anything or anybody other than yourself. But if there's one trait I hope you get, that your Mom and I both share, it's the gift of throwing yourself fully into your circumstances and being involved in the outcome.

Your Mom and I have both taken a lot of risks in our lives, Atlas, and each in our own ways. Yet none of these risks have ever felt close to what I feel with your arrival coming up soon. It feels like we're being given a tremendous blessing, opportunity, and chance to "level-up" this life experience.

You. You're a little bundle of joy, and you've already started to make huge waves of impact in our household.

I love you,
Dad

March 30

Dear Atlas,

It's me, your Dad.

I missed writing to you this weekend because I was spending the days with your Mom and your uncle. You were quite the star! A lot of people stopped to congratulate your Mom, and we spent a lot of time talking about you.

In less than a month, you'll be in our arms. I think your Mom and I are both ready to have you here now. It's like being in the car for a long trip and reaching a point when you're ready to get to your destination.

I've had a lot of time to think about what life will be like when you get here. My best attempts involve taking everything I know now about our life and adding a whole different dimension to it, one where we are both doing things differently than we have in the past.

You're our dependent, Atlas. That also hit home for me, the idea that somebody will fully depend on the two of us. It's our responsibility (and opportunity) to raise you as a human being who has a positive impact on the world around him. From human rights to planetary hygiene, I hope we set a good example for you to follow.

Your pending arrival has helped me understand love differently, Atlas. When I was younger, I listened to a song called "Love Is a Verb," which sang about the action part of love. Having you is one of the ways I've seen love go beyond a feeling.

For example, your Mom and I are practicing ways of communicating with each other, showing each other care, and being proactive about your arrival. Sometimes love looks like a hug and a kiss. Other times, it looks like taking the trash out.

On that note, kiddo, it's time for your Dad to take out the trash and get his day started.

I love you,
Dad

March 31

Dear Atlas,

It's me, your Dad.

Your Mom and I have reached a point when you could easily arrive in days—or weeks.

That uncertainty has been somewhere in the back of my mind at all times. It seems like no matter where I am or what I'm doing, I find you somewhere in my thoughts.

I've been checking in with myself a lot lately, asking myself how ready I feel I am for your arrival. That's a hard question to answer, Atlas. I feel ready for you to be here, but I don't entirely know what it will be like to turn on the "Dad switch."

I grew up watching my Dad, thinking he somehow knew how to be a Dad. During the times he didn't live up to my expectations, I was disappointed. Now, I find myself in the same position he was in: expecting you, making the switch to providing for somebody other than myself, and feeling the urge to get sustainable work that our family can depend on for years to come.

Feeling how I feel now, I realize I probably could have cut my Dad a lot more slack for all the times he acted like a human instead of a hero. After all, that's what we all are, Atlas. We're people, and sometimes we act like it.

One of the things I hope we embody as a family is the ability to accept each other when we act like human beings, when we spill the wine, run late, forget to do something, and disturb each other in the middle of the night.

It's a relief to even type these things to you, Atlas. Because I realize it's a lot easier to accept these things as part of life than to develop anxieties or anger about them.

Your Mom and I can't wait to meet you, Atlas. It's time for your Dad to get to work.

I love you,
Dad

April 1

Dear Atlas,

It's me, your Dad.

The moments are ticking away until you arrive, and I'm doing a lot of processing. There's a part of me that feels like I somehow missed the bus for "Dad school" and other people know more than I do about what it means to be a parent.

You may feel this way someday. Or perhaps you'll join the ranks of Dads who seem like they were born with a diaper bag in one hand and a bottle in the other.

I think this is part of the process, Atlas. It's also a lot like the life experience I've had so far, always feeling like somebody knows more than I do when I'm in the middle of new and diverse experiences.

Admittedly, things feel clearer on some days than on others. Like when you love someone, there are moments when you're head over heels for your partner. Other moments, you're tripping over your own heels to find space away from them.

Life is a perpetual game of push and pull, Atlas. However, in the middle of that tension is a beautiful place of harmony. Yes, sometimes you wonder if you're in the eye of the storm or safely out of its path. That's okay.

I wish I could tell you I'm prepared to be a Dad—or at least that I feel like I am. I don't, though. And I think it's important for you to know that even your Dad has moments when he doesn't feel like he has it all together.

Someday, though, I know we'll all be sitting at the dining room table, looking out huge windows at the view in front of us, and soaking in the rays of being a family unit that loves each other.

It's all worth it.
Dad

April 2

Dear Atlas,

It's me, your Dad.

Sometimes I don't know where to start when I write to you. Today is one of those mornings. I'm torn between telling you how I feel, talking about the significance of the day (Good Friday), and remarking on how the universe seems to provide for our family ahead of your arrival.

When I was younger, I didn't really understand what my Dad did. I knew he worked on a computer and was the go-to guy for people who didn't understand how to use one. From clients to patrons at our church, Dad helped hundreds of people with their IT needs.

It just dawned on me that you'll never meet your Opa. And that makes me extremely sad because he was one of the most wonderful people I've ever come across in my life. He was helpful, kind, and loving.

He was the type of guy who sincerely tried. While he had his shortcomings (we all do), those aren't the things I remember him for as much as the moments when he made me feel like I was the only person in the universe alongside him.

He will always be my Superman, Atlas. I hope I live in a way that makes you feel the same about me someday, and not just when you're a small child. To a child, every adult seems like a mountain. I hope you still feel this way about me even after you've grown into an adult and experienced your first success, failure, heartbreak, love, and joy.

Heroes still exist, Atlas. Many of them don't wear capes as much as they change diapers, take out the trash, or call their parents and grandparents on a regular basis.

As you get older, you'll understand what I mean.

Love,

Dad

April 3

Dear Atlas,

It's me, your Dad.

Today's Countdown Day for your arrival. Four . . .
three . . . two . . . one . . . you'll be here soon.

Yesterday, your Mom and I met with two of the
women who will help bring you into this world: her
midwife and her doula.

Giving birth with the help of a midwife is a tradition
that not many people follow these days, Atlas. It's
considered unconventional because the birth occurs at
home rather than at a hospital.

Some people choose to face the experience of giving
birth, while others choose to view it as a traumatic
experience that needs heavy anesthesia—which can harm
the child.

When your Mom shared that she wanted to give birth with a midwife, my heart swelled. I knew the type of preparation—and person—it would take to have a natural home birth.

We've both been preparing for you, Atlas, each in our own way. We don't always get it right—nor do I expect we ever will—but we are very, very excited for your arrival.

Love,
Dad

April 6

Dear Atlas,

It's me, your Dad.

I have a lot of hopes for you: hopes for lessons you'll learn, things you'll experience, opportunities you'll have. I hope someday you'll understand what it means to be kind, have the courage to set a boundary, gather the bravery to stick to it, and be willing to unconditionally love and accept others.

Accepting others isn't a hard thing to do, Atlas. It can be boiled down to "live and let live"—a practice that will save you years of stress and anger if you stick to it.

I can change some things in my life, things directly related to my energy field and the way I choose to respond to circumstances. You'll be able to do this, too. Remember that, and it will help you regulate your emotions.

There are times, however, when all the emotional regulation in the world won't work. Or, it will seem to have only worked to a point. I've seen that limit recently and realized that sometimes the best action is to not do anything at all.

Your Mom and I used to feed the birds in the morning. I miss that.

Love,
Dad

April 10

Dear Atlas,

It's me, your Dad.

The older I get, the more experiences I've added to my collection of memories. You, Atlas, are a chapter that I am still experiencing. My life hasn't been the same since I found out you were coming.

There have been a lot of ups and downs, personally, professionally, spiritually, mentally, and in the relationship I have with your Mom. Truth be told, she and I are both doing our best to figure things out, get to know each other, and prepare for a family.

That's a lot to take in, from the outside looking in. However, being in the driver's seat, I see a clear path ahead that involves our whole family. I get worried when I can't see as far ahead as I'd like, or something seems to break down in our proverbial car . . .

As your arrival comes closer, I find more and more things I'm looking forward to experiencing with our family. Walks in the morning, breakfast, Saturday cartoons (none of that post-WWII garbage), love letters for your Mom, your first steps, the sound of your voice . . .

I see memories that were made to be shared and enjoyed by more than two people—family.

Last night, your Mom and I were falling asleep. I put my hand on her so I could feel you. Boy, did you move! I felt our family unit in that moment, as if for the first time. I didn't want to be anywhere else, with anybody else, doing anything other than what I was doing. I felt you, your Mom, and my energy in a harmonious state . . . and it felt like heaven.

I love you,
Dad

April 11

Dear Atlas,

It's me, your Dad.

At this point, you'll be here anytime now. One app says you'll be here in a week. Another doctor says you'll be here in two or three. This is one of those scenarios when only time will tell.

The year leading up to your birth has been a roller coaster. Truth be told, it's one of those stories I wish didn't have to be yours: fighting, anger, hatred, fear, and separation. All the pillars of Hell, from what I've seen.

As one of your parents, I sincerely hope your Mom and I figure things out. I can't imagine our family being separated and depriving ourselves of the beautiful thing that makes life rich: the memories we make with the people we love most.

We're doing our best, Atlas. I can sincerely say that about both your Mom and myself. I don't always like to give her credit for trying. However, I can tell she wants to do the right thing by all of us.

I keep dreaming about you, Atlas. Dreaming of memories we've yet to experience together.

I've seen you walk, smile, laugh, and dance. I've heard your cry, cleaned your throw-up, and changed your diapers.

I love you already. I love you for always.

Dad

April 12

Dear Atlas,

It's me, your Dad.

It's a strange thing to wake up and worry that your best days are behind you. I wish somebody had told me about that chapter of the pre-Dad countdown. In many ways, I think this is a reflection on myself more than on the things I have to look forward to.

I understand these days what it feels like to have back pain, worry about a bill, celebrate a victory, patch a heartbreak, mourn a loss, and feel joy. These things all add up to a lot in my book, each in their own rightful tale.

You, however, are a chapter unknown to me. Despite my dreams of spending time with you, I feel the proverbial corner I'm turning in my life as I become your Father is much larger than I first anticipated.

In many ways I feel somewhat stuck between two present realities: what is and what is to come.

I want to be more than your Dad, Atlas. I want you to someday view me as one of the people who really helped you on your way in this life experience. As you get older, you'll realize the "foundation" of you has been built by many wonderful people. But very few make it into your inner circle and stay there until you're gone.

I lost my Dad, Atlas. Someday you'll see pictures of him. I can't tell you how painful it was to lose my own Dad. Now, I write to you as your Dad—knowing that sometime in the very near future, you and I will share our time together.

Somebody once told me, "I wish I could be the person I was before bad things happened to me."

Right now, you're about to enter the world. It's my job, and your Mom's, to raise you in a home where you are safe, have potential to grow, and don't receive wounds from either of us due to our inability to handle our own pain.

Nothing bad has happened to you, Atlas. And I want to keep it that way—for the rest of your life, if I can.

Love,
Dad

April 13

Dear Atlas,

It's me, your Dad.

For most of my life, I wanted to be really wealthy before I had a family. I grew up in a modest household, and we didn't always have extra money to do the things I wanted to do: play football, buy DJ equipment, or play roller hockey. Boy, did I want to play roller hockey . . .

When I was twelve years old, I learned that the age limit for PADI certification was thirteen. As a result, I called every scuba certification place in town and requested packets of information. Sleek, shiny brochures came in the mail, with advertisements showing people learning how to scuba dive.

I was a dreamer when I was younger, Atlas. I had big dreams in my heart to take the world by force, see amazing sights, and live from the heart. These dreams were fueled by my subscription to *National Geographic Kids,* where Rick the Raccoon would take me on incredible journeys to exotic deserts and ocean reefs.

David Doubilet, a world-renowned underwater photographer, was my hero. I, too, wanted to take beautiful pictures of the universe beneath the waves.

Back then, I thought if I wanted something enough—and put enough bugs in my parents' ears—I would somehow get it.

That wasn't the case for scuba despite my parents' best efforts to keep my interest alive. They bought me a wetsuit, buoyancy compensator, and professional mask and fins from somebody who sold them through a newspaper listing.

I think Mom and Dad spent 95 percent of the money in their bank account to buy me those things, Atlas.

Sadly, that's where my scuba-diving dream stopped. Years passed, and I never got in the water to take my first breath.

As the years went by, I still found a desire to go beneath the waves. However, a fear of sharks came to mind, and I passed up several opportunities when I was in a time, place, or position to get certified.

Almost three years ago, I was working in the tech industry and had a really stable, cushy job. I traveled all over the world, ate the best meals, and saw a part of our world that many will never see, Silicon Valley, from the inside out.

Like the ocean, this world was unlike any other I had seen before. It was fast, fun, exciting, and full of change.

Yet, the entire time, I wasn't happy. I was a part of the machine rather than the driver. And that never really sat well with your Dad.

I got fired, Atlas.

The cards didn't stack in my favor (aided by my own hand), and I soon found myself being told by a teary-eyed boss that I no longer had a position at the company. I was to immediately hand over my laptop computer and exit the building.

It took everything in me to keep the tears inside as I took my final walk down that enormous marble staircase, stepping into the cold Portland air.

As I walked home, I saw one of the regular "friends" I had on the street: a homeless guy, crouched underneath the dryer vent of a hotel. The perfect place to stay warm on a cold winter night in Portland.

Reaching into my wallet, I gave him all the cash I had: a $20 bill. "Enjoy," I said.

"Thank you, brother. God bless you," he said.

God . . . I thought. It's probably time you and I had a conversation . . .

That conversation with God never ended, Atlas.

During that season, I went through a rocky time. I didn't know whether to get a job, start my own business again, or do something completely different—like go to Bali.

Your Great-Opa wrote a book about his life, Atlas. It's an epic tale that is larger than life, a compilation of some of the greatest experiences one man could ever live through in a single lifetime. In Opa's book, he wrote a tale of the day he encountered a fourteen-foot hammerhead shark. I found the island and planned to get into the very same waters.

I wanted to face my fears, Atlas. So, I did. I traveled around the world just to get in the water at Jefman Island and take a quarter-mile swim.

That day, I came alive. So much joy filled my heart once I completed the swim, I felt like I could conquer anything!

That year was a tough one for me, Atlas. I spent the rest of it living in Indonesia, went broke more than a few times, and crash-landed back in the states with $22 in my bank account.

At that time, I had very clear goals that I knew I needed to hit in order to survive. I was determined to find just one client who would pay me $2,500 a month.

Thirty days after landing in the states, I got that client. Next, I wanted to earn $5,000 a month—which I achieved six months later. After that, I wanted to earn $10,000 a month—which I achieved and have maintained to this day.

I tell you all of this because I want you to know that the path leading up to your birth hasn't been an easy one. Nor was it followed by accident.

While your Mom and I have had our share of ups and downs, I can't help but marvel at the supernatural provision that has surrounded us since we learned of your arrival.

When you get older, I hope you have dreams, too. I hope you are raised in a home where you can let these dreams come alive and find yourself as you grow through the process.

I hope you never feel alone, like a failure, or like you don't have options—because you always do.

Love,
Dad

April 14

Dear Atlas,

It's me, your Dad.

Lately, these mornings have felt like a final countdown, even more than usual. I want to feel ready for you, but I admit that I struggle to.

I've wanted more than anything to set a solid example for you to follow. However, I've forged a path that looks a lot more like the one to avoid than the one to follow blindly. I've wrestled with my own focus, sobriety, temperament, and confidence.

I don't know where things will land, Son. I truly don't. You come to me in all of my dreams, in many different shapes and sizes—yet, when I wake up in the morning, I feel like you are a million miles away.

More than anything, I hope your Mom and I are able to make it. The problem is that my confidence in this hope is fading ... fast. If something doesn't change immediately, I fear you'll be reading these letters someday from afar—and I'll be on the other end of the line, hoping you can piece together the full story.

I had so many different ideas of how my life would go, Atlas. Yet, all of those storylines have led your Dad here, to this moment. And I have to trust, trust, trust God in the process that somewhere in this story is a perfect plan, more perfect than any I could have written, imagined, or commanded.

Love,
Dad

April 15

Dear Atlas,

It's me, your Dad.

When I look at the dates on these notes, I realize that the time really is ticking down until you arrive. We've had you predicted to come as early as April 26 and as late as May 2. Your Mom seems to think you'll be here on April 27 or 28. We'll see.

At this point, your Mom and I are eager for you to arrive. There's a part of me that secretly hopes you'll be here after May 1, to be honest with you.

Atlas, I don't know what the world will be like when you're old enough to get your bearings. However, I hope things are in a good place.

As your Dad, I recognize a part of me that sincerely wants to bring you into a better world than the one I entered. However, when I look around, I don't always have confidence that will be the case.

Violence, war, sickness, disease, corruption, and abuse are rampant throughout the world. Sometimes it feels more like walking down the Vegas strip than living on a peaceful planet.

However, I have to remember that all of us are here for a reason, purpose, and time. We chose to be here—I remember doing so. You, too, chose to be here.

And what a time for you to arrive . . .

You'll see.

Love,
Dad

April 17

Dear Atlas,

It's me, your Dad.

Yesterday with your Mom was one of the best days of my life. From the moment we woke up until when we fell asleep, we were in harmony.

Harmony comes in a lot of shapes and sizes, Atlas. Your Mom and I have had a very unconventional road to finding ours.

Whenever I think about our relationship, especially as it involves creating you, I can't help but marvel at the way things have happened. No, Atlas, they have not been conventional in the least. However, they have been good.

Your Mom does something every now and then that I really love: when she sees or hears about something really impressive, she has one word to say, and I love the way she says it.

"Damn."

That's the word I'd use to summarize the journey your Mom and I have had together so far, and as a family. It has been the most beautiful journey I ever could have imagined, full of sunrises, birds, beaches, travel, uncertainty, trust, betrayal, forgiveness, acceptance, and passion.

Our relationship has looked a lot like my paintings, Atlas. Every angle you see them from shows you something new about the piece. As does changing the display and lighting.

What I'm getting at is that the more I look at your Mom, and at us, the more I see different angles, lighting, and depth that were previously unnoticed—and unappreciated.

You coming into our life was one of those angles that changed everything. It felt like a mile marker for both of us, as well as a new standard that we both needed to rise to meet.

Admittedly, Atlas, it's been really hard for me to grow up. I have never really wanted to. However, I'm starting to understand that it's perfectly okay to be a grown-up in some areas of your life, like keeping a steady income, staying healthy, being financially responsible, maintaining relationships, and doing household chores.

Some part of me thought that if I did these grown-up things, I'd somehow lose my inner child. Well, that's not true, Atlas. Your inner child will always be as alive as you allow him to be.

Atlas, I know that if we do things right, our family will go the distance together. I can't think of being anywhere but with you and your Mom as we continue to make our way through this crazy thing called "life in 2021."

Damn.

Love,
Dad

April 18

Dear Atlas,

It's me, your Dad.

Most mornings when I wake up, I step outside to prepare an "offering" for the birds that gather nearby. They're beautiful birds, Atlas—black and blue feathers, the most striking beaks. Whenever I see these birds, I think of you.

I often think about all the memories we will share as Father and Son. That bond is a sacred connection, Atlas. It's one that I take very seriously. I recognize it as my job, along with your Mom, to show you what it means to be a person.

We both have things we hope to teach you as your parents while we experience this life thing together, as a family.

The thing I have to say about your Mom and me is that both of us have lived our lives in really unconventional ways—including all the steps that led to us meeting and having you.

Atlas, I sometimes worry when I look at the way the world is turning. However, I have to remind myself that every step of my life leading up to this point has been perfectly orchestrated, provided for, and led by forces bigger and smarter than myself, and their plans are better than anything I could have come up with.

I love you already, Atlas.

Dad

April 19

Dear Atlas,

It's me, your Dad.

I have a feeling you'll be here this week! Your Mom is ready to hold you in her arms after such a long time carrying you. And I am ready to greet you as your Dad.

A lot of things are changing here, Atlas. I find myself stepping into parent mode even during my day-to-day chores here at the house: getting rid of things I see as choking hazards or objects that might harm you.

I also built a team, Atlas. I built a team of people to work for me so I could spend more time with you and your Mom. Is it scary to spend thousands of dollars to pay employees? Yes, Atlas. It is.

Ever since I was little, I've found ways to make money. It's part of who I am, and I've always viewed earning as a bit of a game: how can I find fun, creative, and interesting ways of making money that maximize my earnings with as little time spent as possible? It's led to an incredible career, Atlas.

I've lived in so many places, explored new cultures, learned valuable skills, and met interesting people from all over the planet (and beyond).

Those adventures are now changing to include you, Atlas. They're changing to prioritize family in a new way, superseding yet including my own work as a priority. Now it's for us and not just me.

My Dad spent a lot of time working. While he sometimes had people who worked for him, mostly he was the man behind the screen, getting things done at one in the morning for clients. I often wished he spent more time with us. Now, I realize I can translate that want into being there for you and your Mom.

You'll learn a lot about me as you get older, Atlas. You'll probably see things in me that I haven't seen (or understood) about myself. I hope one thing you do learn about me is that I value, love, and prioritize family above all else.

I want us to be together. I want a strong family unit because I have seen the strength, support, love, and joy that a loving family unit can provide—because that's how

I was raised. It's also the life I now enjoy with my own family.

That dynamic, more than anything, is something I hope the three (hopefully four) of us can build as we grow together as a family.

I love you, Son.

Dad

April 20

Dear Atlas,

It's me, your Dad.

You're the first thought to cross my mind when I wake up. There is a new consciousness emerging in you, and I'm aware of your entrance in our lives even when I'm still waking up myself.

Every day is a miracle, Atlas. Or, as Sister J used to say, "Every day is a beautiful day, Aaron." That phrase has a whole new meaning to me now that I know you're coming!

Atlas, I'd like to share something with you that comes straight from my heart. It's about your name. As parents, our first gift to you comes in the form of your name. Your Mom and I both knew the strength, value, and meaning that would come from giving you a name.

We wanted something that would be unique, creative, and reflective of your future personality. Your Mom had a few ideas and parameters for your name: it had to start with an A, plus include another A. Two A's—perfect.

I won't ever forget the moment it happened, the time we both looked at each other and agreed to name you Atlas. It felt right. Instantly.

What I want to share with you is where the choice of your middle name comes from. Lucas is the middle name shared by the past four generations of firstborn sons in the Plaat family.

Within that lineage, there was a very strong connection. One could say the love for family has increased dramatically over time, as it truly began with a deficit.

I sincerely want to name you Atlas Lucas Plaat because I want you to know that you share a lineage and history of strong men. They were not perfect, but they did their best, lived outside of their comfort zones, and ultimately put their family first in the lives they lived.

Your Great-Great-Opa was a famous bounty hunter known for hunting with a single bullet.

Your Great-Opa was a war hero and professional motorcycle racer who swam with sharks. He wrote a book about his life, including his love for family and desire to see them grow together.

Your Opa (my Dad) was a family man who found unique ways to spend quality time with each of his six children and my Mom.

As for you, I hope your family is the light of your life, as you will be the light of our household and a great bringer of joy.

I'm proud to be your Dad, Atlas.

Dad

April 21

Dear Atlas,

It's me, your Dad.

This morning, your Mom woke up with sharp pains in her body. "I think I'm having contractions," she said. Immediately, it sunk in that you could be arriving—today.

It seems like the days winding down to your birth have been full of reflection. I have been going through a lot of my personal fears, doubts, questions, and hopes for the life ahead with you.

Truth is, I don't know how to be a Dad. Nobody ever gave me a manual to follow with instructions that would make the task of fatherhood something I could easily learn. No, that's not how things work.

Inside of me is this awakening I can't quite explain. It's a self-illumination that looks at different parts of my life and helps me examine what needs to change. Being a

Dad is a whole different standard than being a bachelor, or even half of a couple—a standard that I've been wrestling with as your arrival draws near.

In a lot of ways, I haven't had to have much accountability for my life, Atlas. Either I don't like accountability, or I've simply believed I had enough self-governance to get along without it. Either way, it's set me back in a lot of areas of my life.

I hope I'm a good Dad for you. I hope I'm a good partner to your Mom. Most of all, I hope I can look at myself in the mirror and know I'm giving it a hundred percent.

Love,
Dad

April 22

Dear Atlas,

It's me, your Dad.

Only yesterday, I realized I've been writing these letters to you from the perspective of being your Dad, without thinking about them from the perspective of you reading them from your Dad.

My Dad wrote me a lot of notes, Atlas. He had his own way of doing it, from commenting on "themes" he graded to sending me countless articles about the newest and latest innovations. He did this with all of his kids because he loved sharing things with us that he knew we'd love.

I don't know when you'll read these notes, Atlas. Truth be told, I don't know how I'll one day present them to you. But I hope we'll be together as a family when it happens.

By this time next week, you'll be in our arms. I know many things will change after the day you arrive, and never quite be the same as they once were. With you, I'm eager to see the changes ahead.

I know what we will be gaining with you, and as a family, is far greater than anything I've surrendered in my life as a bachelor—even one who clings to his old habits . . .

You're coming into a world that is ripe with change, Son. While it seems like there has never been a perfect time to come into the world, I sometimes wonder if life in the 2000s is somehow better or worse than life in another century.

In the story of Superman, his parents (Jor-El and Lara) realized their planet was dying. So, they sent their infant child to earth to have a better life. They packed a ship with the essentials he would need to survive, and then sent him off.

In some ways, I feel like your Mom and I are doing the same thing with you: preparing you for your entrance into a world that desperately needs more good people around. I hope you'll be one of the people who makes that sort of impact on the world around you, even if it takes you a while to arrive at that point in your consciousness.

I want more than just for you to make a positive impact on others, Atlas. I also want you to fully experience the world around you and see it for the beautiful place it can be.

Yes, there are difficult times and stories to read in the news. However, there are also beautiful sunrises, love stories, songs in the dark, and epics to live . . .

I hope you have it all.

Love,

Dad

April 25

Dear Atlas,

It's me, your Dad.

I wonder a lot how life will be when you someday read these notes. I wonder if you'll read all of them or find any joy in knowing your Dad was thinking about you long before you were here.

Sometimes it's hard to write these letters to you. I feel like I don't have a lot to say. Or I feel like there's too much going on in my own head to be able to give you any sort of wisdom. It's hard to feel like I'm doing a good job as your Dad when I feel like I'm drowning, Son.

But then I realize one day you and I will ride in the 944 and have Father-Son talks, as men. It won't matter how old you are, either. I want you to know that you will always be a man to me, your Dad.

Thing is, most of us men are trying to figure out what it means to be a man. Some of us figure out it doesn't involve trucks, guns, or flannel clothing. Others stay in that loop for many years . . .

I'm doing my best to keep my head above water these days, Atlas. I have a lot going on in my mind, and I'm doing my best to make good decisions ahead of your arrival.

Love,
Dad

April 26

Dear Atlas,

It's me, your Dad.

This afternoon, I had an interesting thought about you. I was just finishing some work when I glanced at a painting leaning against the wall. It's one of my recent pieces. I digress.

I thought, I wonder if Atlas will know me.

Not me as your Dad, but the part of me that wrote this letter, the me who existed before diaper changes, parenting, or marriage.

Before I was your Dad, as you know me, I was a young man—just like you. Even now, I don't consider myself grown up quite yet, and a small part of me hopes I never do.

I want you to know I was a young man, full of potential, energy, and personality. I have traveled all over the world, seen my share of exotic cultures, and dove headfirst into a plethora of experiences most people will never even dream about.

I have made huge mistakes, hurting others because I gave them what I had rather than what I now know about life.

I have loved. Oh, how I have loved. I've lived through my heart for thirty-three wonderful years and developed heartfelt connections with many dear friends throughout the world—because I've traveled it.

Atlas, there's going to be a phase of your life when you weave in and out of acceptance of me as your Dad. Some years will be easier for you, and for me, than others, as growing up takes a team effort.

Everything started to change when I found out you were coming. I knew my life wouldn't be what it used to be. However, I knew some of those changes were ready to be present in my life. You, especially.

You'll know me as Dad, Daddy, Papa Bear, or whatever silly name we come up with for me (and you). But that's not how I see myself now because it isn't who I am now, Atlas.

Will you know me as I am now? I don't know. Will you know the young man who loves to ride his motorcycle, listen to Alice Cooper, and toss a beer back

with a cigarette? Some of those parts, I hope you never see
. . .

Other shades of my life will remain for you to uncover and discover as we bond as Father and Son.

You and I may get into fights and disagreements as time goes by. However, I hope you will always know there was once a "me" whom a guy like you hoped he'd someday be like—and I know the "you" who will one day be that man much better than I ever was.

In some ways, a part of me sees the changing tides of my own character, and I hope you, my son, will someday know me as I am now: a stud riding the loudest motorcycle in Tulum, with a louder (and wilder) heart for the ones he loves.

I love you, Son.

Dad

April 27

Dear Atlas,

It's me, your Dad.

I thought you'd be here by now! The anticipation is growing even more now that you're "late" in my mind; I somehow thought you'd be here on the 26th.

The world looks like it's going crazy right now, Son. Conflict and fear seem to be top-of-mind for many people I encounter. News junkies.

At the start of 2020, I made a decision to live from my heart and look fear in the eye. That was when I left Ohio for California, to meet your Mom.

The fear was found in taking that big next step: moving away from a place I was just starting to get comfortable in, the place where I grew up. I crash-landed in Ohio after living overseas in Bali for a year.

Yes, your Dad lived in another country! Several of them.

Before going to Bali, I heard a voice (God, the Universe, or however you deem the Divine) tell me, "Help other people and make beautiful things."

It wasn't the exact advice I was looking for. I'd hoped for something tangible, with clearly defined steps. It was two filters to view the world, two questions to ask myself with every moment I have: "Am I helping others? Am I creating beauty?" That perspective carried me through the next chapter of my life, and ultimately prepared me for your arrival.

You, little Atlas, are the most beautiful thing I have ever seen, felt, and experienced. Even from my limited view of you in your current "home"—which I call the "big ball of love"—in your Mom, I see a miracle in you.

I hope you come into this world and already feel that you are loved, adored, wanted, and respected.

You are.

Love,
Dad

April 28

Dear Atlas,

It's me, your Dad.

As I write to you, I'm looking out of my bedroom window at the beautiful Tulum jungle. Every morning, the trees here fill with an array of birds. Woodpeckers, toucans, parrots, vultures, and exotic birds I haven't yet identified fill the sky.

Nature is one of life's biggest treasures, Atlas. As human beings, it's our job to protect, appreciate, care for, and understand the world around us.

When I was younger (though I could easily write "your age"), my parents got all of us wildlife field manuals. Small, leather-bound books, they were full of vibrant, colorful pictures that identified different types of species. Spiders, insects, plants, and birds were a few that I remember.

My Dad bought us a digital microscope, which we used to study insects, plants, and even our own food. Have you ever seen a fly leg at 400X? Let's do it.

I share this with you because I hope you will discover your own unique love of nature and immerse yourself in it as you get older.

Your Great-Opa wrote a book about his life, which you will someday read. At the end, he wrote a short poem that told where to find him long after he had passed: in the wind, forest, trees, and sun.

You, too, are eternal, Atlas. We all are, in our own unique way.

I love you, Atlas. I keep seeing you in my dreams and I can't wait to hold you in my arms.

Love,
Dad

April 29

Dear Atlas,

It's me, your Dad.

You've kept me and your Mom on our toes this week; we've been expecting your arrival any day now and are excited for you to finally get here.

I was thinking yesterday about how it will feel to hold you in my arms. Normally, I try to pass a newborn baby away to their mother as quickly as I can. But it's going to be different with you because you're my Son.

I hope you never grow up feeling like you are *our* Son. It's really more the other way around, Atlas. We are *your* parents. You picked us. When I think about things that way, it reminds me how much of an opportunity this experience will be to practice patience, humility, and understanding with you.

A lot of parents seem to take a dictator approach with their child, ordering them around, demanding they follow a strict schedule, and pushing them down predefined paths of education, sport, business, and culture.

There are a lot of things I hope you get to discover in your life. However, that's only if you want to discover them. Ultimately, this life thing is entirely up to you once your Mom and I complete this upcoming stage when we provide for, care for, and support you for the next eighteen (or more) years.

Atlas, this moment feels surreal. It's 7:56 a.m. in Tulum. The sun is shining through our living room windows (floor to ceiling glass!) and has landed on the beautiful flower arrangements your Mom placed throughout the room.

We're ready for you, Atlas. In our hearts, and our home.

Love,
Dad

April 30

Dear Atlas,

It's me, your Dad.

These past few days have felt like weeks. Your Mom and I both thought you'd be here by now, but it looks like there are still several days (or even weeks) left.

Looking back at the entire journey of your gestation, I feel at peace knowing you'll be here soon. The peace comes from knowing all of this effort was worth it because you're worth it.

I think a lot about all the moments and memories you and I will inevitably share as Father and Son. On the one hand, I think of the "big" memories; major life events, firsts, and even our goodbyes.

However, life happens in the little moments. And those little moments should never be underestimated, Atlas.

Just like somebody can fall in love with one glance, life has a lot of beauty in the moments between the moments.

It's little things that swell my heart, like when your Mom just came into the room and asked me to open a food container for her.

You'll find this out when you get older, but it means a lot for a man to feel useful. It's the equivalent of feeling sexy—only way better, because you're *doing something.*

Atlas, I often struggle to feel like I've made the best choices in life. Sometimes regret overtakes me, I look back at choices only I can recall, and the pain is overwhelming. Today isn't one of those days.

I look at you, cradled beautifully inside of your Mother, and realize how perfectly my life has aligned to come to this point.

I'm falling in love all over again. This time, it's with you—and our new family.

Love,
Dad

May 1

Dear Atlas,

It's me, your Dad.

It's hard for me to believe that you still haven't arrived, and that you're coming at the same time.

Every morning, I wake up and step away from our bed to sit by the window and write you these notes while I stare at the jungle. It's magical, Atlas. I couldn't have asked for a more perfect backdrop (both figuratively and literally) for your arrival or for the time needed before you came, to prepare.

Something I've noticed your Mom doing before your arrival is making our home beautiful. She's set up beautiful flower arrangements all over the house, scented the air with Ayurvedic essential oils, and carefully stocked us with everything we need for you.

Atlas, one of the most important things in life is family. However, the environment and way you are raised have a strong impact on your relationship and contribution to the family dynamic.

Your Mom and I hope to raise you to be a respectful, courteous, kind, compassionate, caring, loyal, strong, forgiving, peaceful, and wise young man.

See, it's not my place to want specific things for you, such as an occupation, interests, or even likes/dislikes. That's all for you to find out as you get older. I do want certain attributes for you because I know that, whoever you turn out to be, you'll be a better person if you're full of character, integrity, and true grit.

True grit comes in different packages, Atlas. Sometimes it looks like persisting through a tough time, carrying an engine, or achieving a goal. Other times, true grit looks like being faithful to your partner (eyes, brain, hands, and heart) or choosing love over fear.

It takes a great deal of courage to be your own person, Atlas.

We live in a world where it's a lot easier to be a sell-out and wear a label, take a job, make a car payment, or live behind the screen to avoid discovering who you really are on the inside.

There's one thing I know about you, Atlas. It's that you will have a big heart and light up the world for the people around you—just like you do for your Dad.

Love,
Dad

May 2

Dear Atlas,

It's me, your Dad.

I'm living an experience now that I wish more people took the time to capture and reflect on: the moments before becoming a Father.

Fatherhood is a very special gift, Atlas. It's a responsibility that I wish a lot more men took upon themselves to do well. It's not an easy undertaking because it's not something you get to practice or repeat.

Being a Dad is a one-shot thing. Either you get it right, or you don't. At thirty-three years old, I've seen the impact proper parenting can have.

Good parenting results in healthy children, Atlas. In my home, our parents were keenly focused on maintaining harmony. I don't mean they kept the place quiet. Rather, they consciously put effort into helping their children realize the value of their siblings and grow strong relationships with them.

That's the bonus of parenting. You get to see your children succeed, while also forming unbreakable bonds with their own kin: friendship, accountability, trust, support, laughter and even vice.

I've seen and done a lot of cool, exotic, and flashy things in my life, Atlas. I've traveled the world, eaten thousand-dollar meals, and driven exotic cars. I've dined with billionaires, millionaires, beggars, and outcasts . . . that list could go on. Yet, all of those experiences don't add up to the excitement, and permanence, of being your Dad.

I know you will be here soon, little Atlas.

Love,
Dad

May 3

Dear Atlas,

It's me, your Dad.

The weekend has come and gone without your arrival. I thought for sure you'd be here by now, and it has been a bit straining (emotionally) to stretch out the wait, especially for your Mom.

We've been talking a lot lately about our own upbringings and the way we hope to raise you. A family environment has to be healthy in order for all members to thrive. How do you define a healthy family?

That's a great question, Atlas. I see a healthy family as a unit in which each member feels like they are wanted, loved, contributing, heard, and understood. These are the "roots," if you will.

I also see a healthy family as one that shares mutual respect, laughs and cries together, encourages and uplifts each other, holds each other accountable, helps others, and serves the poor.

There's a saying that you can tell a tree by the fruit it bears. I hope our family tree is full of everlasting fruit, the kind that leaves a legacy long after we leave this plane[t].

You, Atlas, are one of those legacies. Throughout the pregnancy, I've wrestled with the permanence of the situation, feeling as if there is a perpetual hourglass dropping the sands of your arrival.

I see every action and thought now connected to both you and your Mom. Now, I want to live for a lot more than just myself. That's the part inside of me that I see changing the most.

For most of my life, I've only had to worry about myself. There was a void of accountability and I lived pretty recklessly; life was one huge pendulum swinging between pleasure and pain.

Now that I know you're coming (and almost here), I know my life now counts for more than just me: it's you, your Mom, and this new unit we are all creating called our family, which will support, provide, and nurture all of us—if we are good to it.

You (and your Mom) are one of the most important pieces of something my heart wants the most: a home. I hope you never forget that, Atlas. I know you and your Mom won't as long as I treat you that way.

Ahead of being your Dad, I want you to know that I feel like I don't yet know how to be one; I don't yet have diaper bag lightning reflexes, and my changing skills feel a bit rusty. But I'm going to give being your Dad one hundred percent, and that means knowing when to get out of my own way.

Our new family unit is like a three-legged table, Atlas. All three of us are standing on it, and each leg belongs to us to care for. If one leg suffers, we all fall. We need each other.

I don't just love you, Atlas. I need you, just like I need your Mom and she needs me. Necessity means you don't dispose of something, but protect and cherish it.

Get here soon, little Atlas.

Love,
Dad

May 4

Dear Atlas,

It's me, your Dad.

The time leading up to your arrival has continued to dwindle as the days go by. Your Mom and I both thought you would be here a long time ago, and the wear and tear has begun to accumulate.

I don't know how other people go through pregnancy, Atlas. From what I've heard other people say, paired with what I've heard us tell others, I don't think people are really transparent about the journey of pregnancy.

As your Dad, I've experienced countless moments when I've had to process my deepest fears, worries, anxieties and pain. I've had to look deep into the proverbial mirror at my own soul, realizing it will directly impact the direction yours takes.

I want to give you a safe home environment, Atlas—the kind of place where you always feel safe to be yourself. I want you to live in a place where you never see your parents fight. Ever. I want you to know that your laughter and smiles are just as welcome to us as your tears and frowns.

I've wrestled a lot in my life with feeling good enough. Son, it's one of the worst feelings and one of the hardest to overcome because it makes you feel like there's something wrong with you. I wish I had been able to convey this to my parents and tell them how I felt, because I couldn't articulate it until I was an adult.

When you get older, you'll find that some parts of you don't really feel grown-up. Pay attention to those parts, Atlas. It's important to understand which parts of yourself need to be seen, appreciated, and treated like a young child.

This is especially important for your emotions, Atlas. Try giving an adult the grace, love, and compassion you would give a child when they are upset. It's drastically different from treating them like an adult, which implies they somehow "knew better."

I don't have any expectations for you, Atlas. Rather, I am holding my arms wide open for whoever you are, whatever you want to become, and however you choose to do it.

I'm your Dad, and one of the best co-pilots you'll ever have on your journey, if you allow me to be.

Love,
Dad

May 5

Dear Atlas,

It's me, your Dad.

Many years ago, I remember waking up and deciding I wouldn't have "bad days" anymore. They seemed like an unnecessary waste of energy. So, I opted to make every day a great one and find the positive in it.

I've done my best to carry that approach forward with me as I get older, Atlas. These days, I remind myself how many things I have to be grateful for, and I realize that every day is only as good as I make it.

You will have your moments, though, Atlas. You'll have days when you feel stretched too thin, out of options, frazzled, dazzled, and late. Those days are the ones that build your character and harden your mettle.

As your Dad, it's my job to help you navigate these moments by setting an example of how I conduct myself during the times that inevitably beset us all. Observation is the ultimate teacher.

I grew up in a home where I never once saw my parents fight, call each other names, hit each other, or use profanity. When disagreements with siblings happened, we were instructed on how to quickly forgive, hug, and get back to normal.

That was an invaluable asset, Atlas. I learned how to treat other people well through the readily available vehicle of multiple siblings.

That's the kind of home I hope you are raised in. I hope you never hear fighting, name-calling, abuse, threats, or disrespect. Those things are poisonous and unnecessary, and they have no place in our home.

As your Dad, I want more than anything to protect you from these things. I don't want you to grow up feeling like you deserve to be disrespected because that's the behavior you saw in your own home.

I wish a lot more parents recognized one simple thing: when they don't figure their pain, problems, or karma out, they multiply those issues and dump them on their children.

Some people grow up and never realize the problems they face aren't theirs. Those problems belong to their parents, who gave their children what they had. Sometimes that isn't a lot.

I'm doing my best, Atlas.

Love,
Dad

May 6

Dear Atlas,

It's me, your Dad.

I sometimes wonder if every child is born with pure ideals and hopes. As children, we are born innocent into this plane[t] and crafted by the experiences we encounter as we grow older.

When I was younger, I felt heavy disappointment when I was wronged. It felt like double pain to receive a blow from somebody, then feel deep disappointment inside because what happened shouldn't have happened. I felt a love lost for the world and a dwindling of my hopes that others would be faithful, trustworthy, and kind.

In my twenties, I learned a short phrase that helped me through these difficult moments, a phrase that helped me understand I wasn't the problem: "People give you what they have."

From dollars to donuts, this is how life works. You can apply this wisdom by reminding yourself that in every encounter with other people, they have a certain bandwidth for what they can give you.

Some people truly don't have it in them to be kind. The universe needs those people to be the pain of other people's day, because it makes the moments of kindness that much more appreciated.

I hope you are the type of person who lights up other people's day, Atlas. That's probably more from my side of things. I hope you treat other people with respect, dignity, courtesy, and patience.

The world desperately needs good people right now, Atlas. I hope you are one of them.

Love,
Dad

May 7

Dear Atlas,

It's me, your Dad.

I recently paused to wonder if you'll know me for who I am. Then, it struck me that you won't know me for who I have been unless I share those things with you.

My Dad told me a lot of stories about his life. From playing football as a young man to graduating from The Ohio State University, he had a unique life path; since he worked as a self-employed entrepreneur for his entire adult life, I never saw my Dad work a regular job.

I followed in his footsteps, Atlas. I've never found a job that suited me and have chosen to live as a self-employed entrepreneur. There are a lot of ups and downs with the occupation, but the benefits far outweigh the negatives.

Ahead of your arrival, I'm especially glad to have this occupation. I know that I'll have the freedom, flexibility, and time in my schedule to be a good Dad to you and for you.

I've never had a traditional life, Atlas. As far back as I can remember, I did things differently than the rest. I guess a lot of that can be attributed to my upbringing as well as my personality.

I've always had one eye ahead of me, never quite fully present. Ahead of being your Dad, I've realized that it's okay to be in the moment. Now, especially, I cherish these moments of peace, quiet, and clarity.

In these final days until you arrive, I think a lot about what kind of example I'm going to set for you. I wonder how my actions will impact your upbringing (a lot) and what personal issues I need to work on, separate from you.

Atlas, this pregnancy has been a journey. It has been one my greatest challenges yet. I haven't always acted as gracefully as I would like or thought things through as much as they needed to be. I did my best, Atlas. Even in moments when it didn't feel like it.

Pregnancy is very much a solo journey for both the Mom and the Dad. She is going through her transformations, and I am also going through my own.

Those journeys are leading us both to you, Son. We have a choice to make, as your parents, of how we will continue this journey as a family. I hope your arrival sparks something new in each of us, where we can see life, each other, our future, and the present with new eyes that previously hadn't been used.

I'm praying for a miracle, Atlas. I'm praying for the miracle of our family.

We can't do it without you.

Love,
Dad

May 8

Dear Atlas,

It's me, your Dad.

One of my favorite things in life is waking up early on a Saturday morning. Saturday feels like a day of rest, and the early morning hours feel especially free when nobody else is awake.

I'm looking outside now at the beautiful jungle surrounding our home. Birds are flying through the air, which is filled with the sound of their calls.

Soon, you and I will be sharing these moments together. We'll sit at the windowsill and watch as the birds come down to eat the little pieces of food I'll place on the edge of our balcony. Those moments, Atlas, are the priceless treasures I look forward to in parenting.

Truth be told, the whole parenting process is a treasure. I know all of the moments may not be as soft and sweet as the idea of feeding morning birds, but I think there will be more than enough joy in your face to help me never lose sight of what's important.

Your Uncle Mark had a dream about you yesterday! He said he was present for your birth and you came out a very happy, smiling child. You also looked just like me, he said.

We'll find out soon. Very soon.

I love you,
Dad

May 9

Dear Atlas,

It's me, your Dad.

Throughout your pregnancy, I've gone on my own inner journey of reflection, growth, and processing. In nine months, you can process a lot.

Before I was old enough to buy a beer, I lost my Dad (your Opa) to Cancer. He was fifty-one years old, Atlas. He was my original Hero, followed by my Opa, his Dad. Life is difficult to figure out in your twenties. It's a lot harder when you lose your Dad on top of it.

In the last weeks before your arrival, I've battled a lot of difficult emotions. Fear is present, as well as its cousins, doubt and uncertainty. Most of these emotions seemed normal to process. It made sense to me, as an emerging Father, that I would need to battle a few demons before your arrival.

However, there was one bit of pain that didn't seem to go away. It felt familiar, as if the pain has been inside of me for years. Yet, it felt infinitely multiplied ever since finding out I was to be your Dad.

What was that pain, Atlas? I figured out the answer to that question last night.

Not all pain shows its source right away, Atlas. More importantly, people experiencing it don't always know where the source is and often make mistakes, especially when dealing with other people fighting to do the same thing.

People often treat their pain in the wrong way, as well, such as by using alcohol, drugs, career, distraction, sex, toys, speed, and more pain to cover up their wounds instead of heal them. That's why you see so many young men joining gangs: rather than address their issue of having no father, they try to replace what's missing and mask their tears with fakes instead of fathers.

I think people do this with God, too, Atlas. They try to replace, repair, or cover up the painful parts of their spirit with their own fixes instead of allowing God to step into those spots and fill the void.

My answer to the source of the deep-rooted pain came when I realized that the heroes I looked up to in my life for all things related to being a Dad (and man) are no longer alive—your Opa and Great-Opa, to me, Dad and Opa.

I'm in that spot now for you, Atlas. Dad. Daddy. Father. And I feel somewhat lost as I am embarking on this journey, because I miss these men. I miss *my* Dad, Atlas.

It's been thirteen years and the pain has never gone away, though I have done my best to deal with it or mask it.

I tried my best, Atlas. I tried to "be a man" and become successful. So, I threw myself headfirst into projects and chased the everlasting dollar. The money never kept me warm at night or told me how much it appreciated me being me. As a result, I made it all and lost it several times over before I turned thirty.

Somewhere along the lines, I discovered that being a man meant a lot more than having a BMW in your garage. It meant living from your heart, keeping your word, giving to the poor, calling your family (and supporting them), living courageously, and respecting others. I realized that taking out the trash makes you just as much a hero as launching an IPO—especially when your partner is pregnant.

You'll learn as you grow older that some pain is meant to be there for a reason. It's okay that I miss my

Dad, Atlas. Someday, you will also understand what this means. However, between the pain you will experience in your life and its inverse of abundant joy, you will find a balance—and yourself somewhere in the middle of it all.

Our bags are packed for the hospital (just in case), and we are both as ready for you as we will ever be.

Get here soon, little Atlas. I can't wait to hold you in my arms. Already, I can't imagine the feeling of letting go after holding you for the first time.

You. Our little Hero.

Love,
Dad

May 10

Dear Atlas,

I don't need to tell you who I am anymore because you can see me now with those big, beautiful eyes of yours. You were born yesterday, after only four hours of labor, in Playa Del Carmen, Mexico.

After all these months, seeing you with my own eyes was inexplicably beautiful, wonderful, and peaceful, though the process of welcoming you into this world was inarguably one of the most strenuous experiences of my life, despite your Mom being the one who did the work to deliver you.

Your Mom and I worked as a team to get you out safely. She did the pushing, and I was there to hold her, rub her back, and let her hang with her arms around my neck when the contractions came.

They happened. Fast. It was as if you wanted to come into the world after so many weeks and months of keeping us waiting. And come you did, little Atlas. From the moment we could see the top of your head coming out of your Mom, you were surrounded by love, encouragement, and the best medical staff and facilities I've ever seen.

I will never forget the moment you arrived. Your Mom was having a contraction, and she was struggling with the tremendous pain that comes with labor.

"I can't do this," she said. "God, please help me." She went through contraction after contraction.

She was interrupted by the midwife, who asked, "Would you like to feel his head?"

Your Mom reached down with her hand and touched your head for the very first time. Thirty seconds later, she gave one final push and I watched you slide right out of her as I stood behind her with encouragement, back rubs, and cheering.

I stood in the room as I heard you cry for the first time. You filled the air with soft cries as you took your first breath.

Many people told me before you arrived that the moment I stared into your eyes, my entire life would change and I would never be the same.

They were right, Atlas. After looking into those beautiful brown eyes of yours for the first time in my life, I saw my own reflection staring back at me. You. The most beautiful little baby I've ever seen in my life.

Shortly after you were born, your Aunt Julia sent me a video of herself singing a lullaby for you. She based it on "Dear Theodosia," a song from the Broadway musical *Hamilton.*

Stroking her ukulele, she sang the very first song your ears ever heard.

> Dear Atlas, what to say to you?
> You have my eyes, you have your mother's name
> When you came into the world, you cried
> And it broke my heart
> I'm dedicating every day to you
> Domestic life was never quite my style
> When you smile, you knock me out, I fall apart
> And I thought I was so smart
> You will come of age with our young nation
> We'll bleed and fight for you
> We'll make it right for you
> If we lay a strong enough foundation
> We'll pass it on to you, we'll give the world to you
> And you'll blow us all away

Someday, someday

Yeah, you'll blow us all away

Someday, someday

Oh, Atlas, when you smile I am undone

My son, look at my son

Pride is not the word I'm looking for

There is so much more inside me now

Oh Atlas, you outshine the morning sun

My son

When you smile, I fall apart

And I thought I was so smart

My father wasn't around

My father wasn't around

I swear that I'll be around for you

I'll do whatever it takes

I'll make a million mistakes

I'll make the world safe and sound for you

Will come of age with our young nation

We'll bleed and fight for you

We'll make it right for you

If we lay a strong enough foundation

We'll pass it on to you, we'll give the world to you

And you'll blow us all away

Someday, someday

Yeah, you'll blow us all away

Someday, someday

I'm watching your Mom feed you right now. You, perfectly beautiful and innocent in her arms, lovingly bonding with the woman who has carried you for nearly a year.

In this moment, I'm starting to understand the dramatic shift that takes place when a child is born. Specifically, I understand the transformation a man goes through when he holds his firstborn son in his arms, looking through the lens of countless generations that have persisted, beaten the odds, and survived this thing called life.

You and I are both part of that journey now, Atlas. It all began the moment you were born, and it will continue on for many legacies long after you and I take our final dirt nap.

I don't know where this journey will lead, Atlas. However, I want you to know that, after seeing you with my own eyes, I now understand the great responsibility (and gift) that being a Father is.

Now that you're here, our family has been born, and it's up to us to raise, teach, discipline, love, care for, provide for, and protect you. As your Dad, it's my job to take on these responsibilities for our entire family.

Atlas, I promise you that I will make a million mistakes. Nobody gets it right one hundred percent of the time. However, I want you to know I will do my very best to be your Dad and a loving partner to your Mom.

Until the wheels come off, baby.

Love,
Dad

Epilogue

For most of my life, I've wondered what it would feel like to be a Dad. Growing up in a house with six children, I often wondered if I was cut out for family life or if I would be one of those people who never quite make it to the point of having a family. To be transparent, I spent most of my twenties thinking I wouldn't have one of my own.

Yet, typing this as I look into Atlas's eyes, I now see life through a different lens: the perspective of no longer living a life that's all about yours truly.

Many people told me ahead of being a Dad that I wouldn't ever be able to imagine life without my family. Now, I understand what they were talking about. When I look into his eyes, I see something I have waited thirty-three years to help create and bring into this world.

Looking back, I see the fears and trepidations I had about raising a family were well warranted. In fact, I'm glad to have spent so many years dreading the possibility of having a family, because it helped prepare me for the day when I finally became a Dad.

My fears? Money. Time. My sense of me-ness that I worried would be lost. I wasn't raised in a family with a ton of extra money, and every little bit counted. As a result, I grew up fearing that I, too, would someday struggle to afford a family. I worried that being unable to provide as I would like to would somehow negate my ability to be a good Dad, or would disqualify me.

When I was younger, my Dad often reminded me to "use the right tools for the job" when I set my hands to a task. More often than not, this advice was given after he caught me using a screwdriver as a hammer, something it was never intended to be used for.

Ahead of Atlas's arrival, I had many moments when I sat down with myself and soul-searched to figure out what "tools" I have available to be a Dad. The answers came quickly, as I realized my parents did an incredible— beyond incredible—job of raising their children.

They didn't just raise their children, either. They did so much more than that for each of us. They taught us how to think, find answers, support ourselves, and contribute to the world around us with our talents.

God has given me a lot of talents. However, just like the parable of the man who left his servants for several years, giving each of them "talents" (units of currency) ahead of his departure, he tasked them with one thing: "Do something with what I gave you."

The man left on a long journey, and returned after several years. When he returned, he met with each of his servants and asked what they'd done with the fortunes they received.

The first, given the largest sum, responded, "I took the money you gave me, invested it, and now have double the amount to return to you."

"Well done, thou good and faithful servant."

He asked the second how they had spent the money.

"Master, I took the talents you gave me, purchased several fields, and now how have double the money to return to you."

"Well done, thou good and faithful servant," the master replied.

Lastly, he came to the third servant, who was given the smallest amount of money. When probed about how the funds were used, the servant replied, "Master, I know you are a hard master. You produce things where nobody else can. You make fortunes where others go poor. I feared that I wouldn't be able to use the money as well as you could have, so I buried it in a field, and here it is for you."

The master was furious. "You fool!" he said. "You could have given this to the money lenders, and they would have returned interest to you. Instead, what I gave you is now worth less than it was when I left."

The servant looked at the master, knowing he had made a grave mistake.

The master continued. "Get away from me, you unworthy servant. I never knew you." He banished the errant servant from the property, then took that money and gave it to the first servant as a reward for his faithfulness.

The lesson here is that when I was a young man, I, too, was given talents and abilities, from the ability to make money in creative ways to my writing ability. As the years have gone by, I've done my absolute best to be faithful with the tools, resources, network, support system, and talents I've been blessed with.

Now, staring into the eyes of my firstborn son, I have peace in my heart knowing the years ahead of his arrival have been spent well. Similar to how a potter works clay into a sculpture, my life has been a transformative process that I feel very lucky to be a part of.

When I look at Atlas, I see the remarkable gift that life is. In his eyes I see a reflection of my own, and it helps me understand the tremendous amount of care, grace, forgiveness, love, and support I must offer not only my son, but myself and others as well.

I will admit it's difficult to show yourself love and care. Sometimes God sends other people into your path who need the love you haven't shown yourself or known how to. In my life, I have had countless individuals cross my path who have helped me understand what it means to slow down, be patient, and understand that everybody needs somebody sometimes, myself included.

This book came as a result of one morning when I woke up and thought long and hard about the impending future of being a Dad. Will I be a good one? I thought.

That was when I looked back at my own life and thought about my own Dad's shortcomings with his family. The biggest hurt was that he made promises he couldn't keep—to me, my siblings, and our Mom.

I wondered how I would overcome the fear of repeating his mistakes. That's when the idea of writing letters to Atlas struck me. It dawned on me that I could find one small way, every day, to show Atlas that he's loved, wanted, and thought of long before he took his first breath.

That's when *Dear Atlas* was born. I took out my iPad and began a folder to hold the notes I would write and started to write him every morning before beginning my workday.

Now, I look back at these notes and realize that a little legacy has been left for Atlas. Long before he will even be able to read these notes, they will have been read by countless others across the world, who I hope will find the same inspiration, love, and encouragement I offered him with my words.

The story is far from over. In fact, it's only now just beginning. Looking back at 2020, I wish I could have spoken these words to myself:

Dear Aaron,

It's me, your future self. I'm staring at your beautiful son right now, and I wanted to take a moment to share a few things with you.

You're probably freaking out right now. That's fine. Pregnancy is a big deal. However, I want you to know that you've got all the tools, abilities, talent, network, and love to be an incredible Dad, provider for your home, and partner.

I want you to know that when Atlas is here, you will have everything you need in order to provide for him—down to the tiniest of details. You will work hard, grow your client base, and finally start the process of being your own client.

I probably won't be able to send this entire message to you from where I am. So, I want you to know one last thing, if nothing else:

It's all worth it.

You'll be a great Dad, too.

Love,

You

Made in the USA
Columbia, SC
22 July 2024